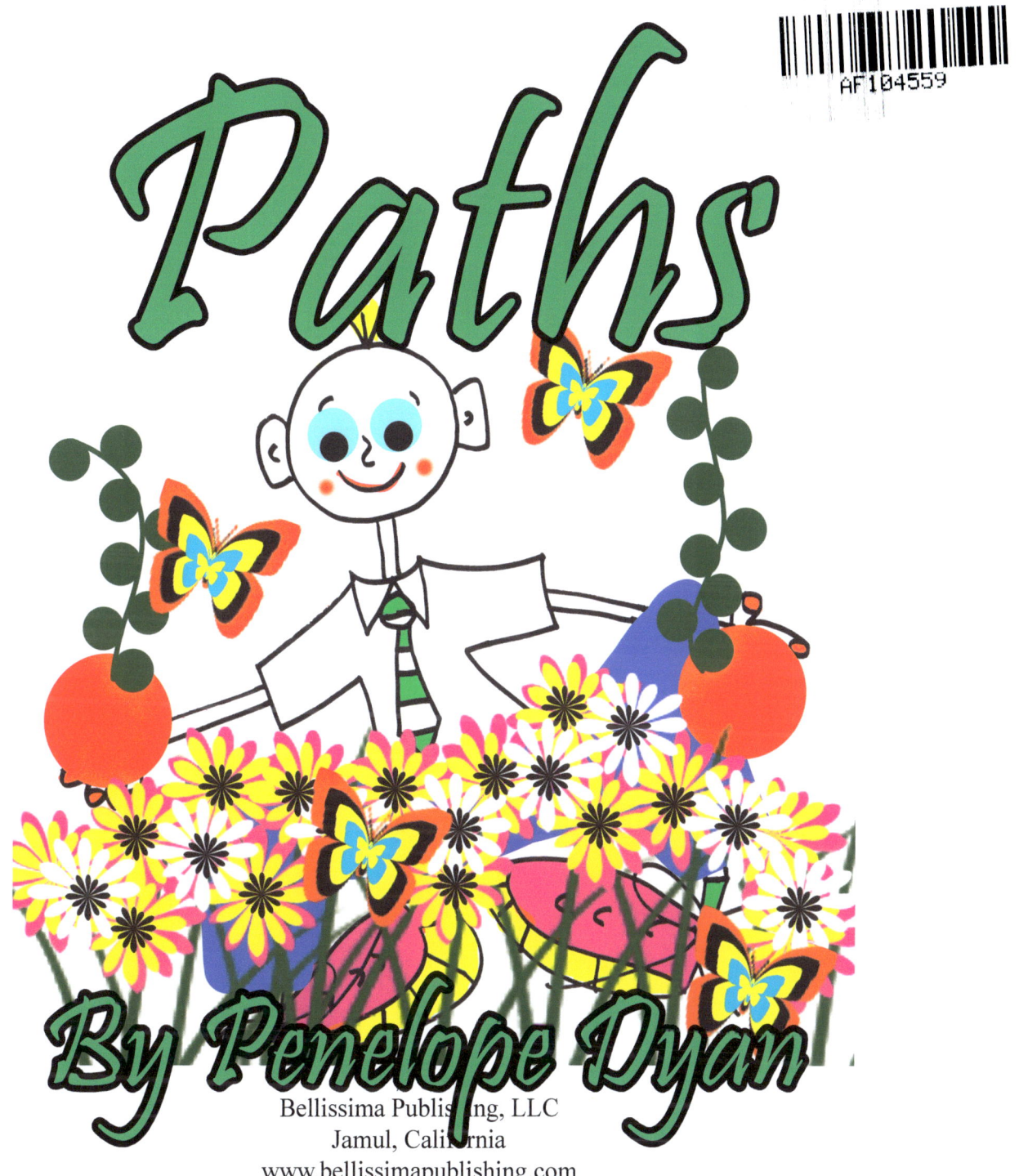

Paths

By Penelope Dyan

Bellissima Publishing, LLC
Jamul, California
www.bellissimapublishing.com

Copyright © 2022 by Penny D. Weigand

All rights reserved. No part of this book may be
reproduced or transmitted in any form or by any means,
electronic or mechanical, including photocopying,
recording, or by any other means, or by any information or
storage retrieval system, without permission from the publisher.

ISBN 978-1-61477-603-1
First Edition

"Think carefully about what you do in life and about where you go!"

Penelope Dyan

Introduction

We all have to choose our own path in life, and that also means choosing between doing what is right and doing what is wrong. And, of course, we should always choose what is right. But sometimes that may seem like a difficult choice, because sometimes temptation is strong. But the truth is you must always choose your own path, and nobody can do that for you.

Think about this as you travel through the pages of this fun, 'learn to read' book written and illustrated by award winning author, attorney and former teacher, Penelope Dyan, that is filled with word recognition, word repetition and rhyme, all to help a kid build his or her reading skills and reading word vocabulary, as he or she had fun learning! Fun? Yes! Because learning should always be (and must always be) fun or a kid simply won't love to learn!

And when you are all finished traveling through the pages of this fun, 'learn to read' book, you can go to Bellissimavideo's YouTube channel; and you can watch the free music video that goes with this book and have even more learning fun!

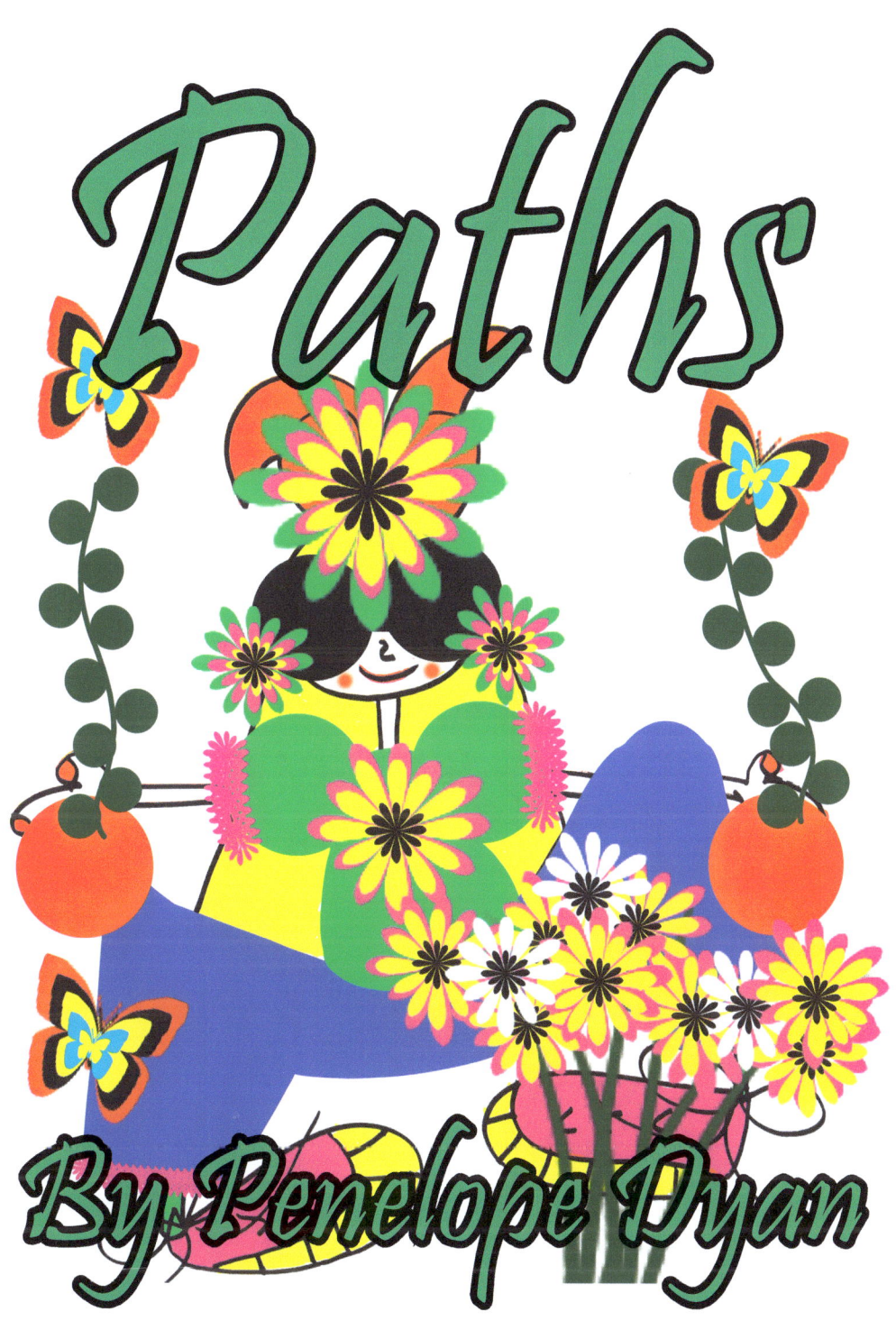

I came to a crossroads in my life!
AND I (quite simply) did NOT know
which path I should take
OR where I should go!
And so, I asked my dear, sweet mother
what I should do!
AND she (quite simply) simply told me,
"What path you take in life
is (quite simply) simply up to YOU!"
And THEN, she said,
"When you come to a crossroads in life
no one can, or should, EVER tell you
which path YOU should take TAKE!
Because the answer to that question
a decision only YOU can MAKE!"

My friend, the elephant, told me
what my mother said to me that day
was (and is) very, very, VERY true!
And I would (quite simply)
simply listen to the elephant
if I just happened to be YOU!
Because, you see . . .
the elephant never, never ever forgets!
And the elephant never, never ever lies!
And my friend, the elephant,
ALSO happens to be
oh so very, very, VERY wise!

And the oh so very, very, VERY
handsome, tall giraffe said
with my dear, sweet mother
he absolutely,
one hundred percent,
really, truly (and quite simply)
simply HAD to agree!
And so did the monkey
sitting oh so very, very, VERY
high, high, HIGH up
(eating apples)
In the old, old, OLD apple tree!

The smiling cow said,
"With the elephant, the giraffe,
your dear, sweet mother,
and the monkey sitting
oh so high, high, HIGH up
(eating apples)
in the old, old, OLD apple tree,
I really, truly, absolutely
(quite simply)
simply have to agree!"
And the sheep told me
the very, very, VERY same thing!
And the bird agreed!
And the bird began to SING!

The prancing horse (of course)
(quite simply)
simply HAD to agree
AND so did the hippopotamus!
And so did
the busily, buzzing, bumble bee!

And my brother and my father
agreed with my mother,
right along with ALL of the rest!
Because, as everyone
(quite simply) simply knows,
my mother always, always ALWAYS
really, truly, absolutely,
AND one hundred percent
(quite simply) simply knows
exactly and precisely
exactly what is always, always best!

And the mermaid,
and ALL of the fish
in the deep, deep, deep blue of the sea,
told me they really, truly,
absolutely
and one hundred percent,
with my mother just had to agree . . .
right along with ALL of the rest,
including the monkey
(sitting and eating apples)
oh so high, high, HIGH up
in the old, old, OLD apple tree!

And my very, very, VERY best friend
also (quite simply) simply said
with my mother SHE had to agree . . .
right along with the elephant,
and the giraffe,
the mermaid and the fish,
the cow and the sheep,
my brother and my father,
the hippopotamus and the horse,
AND the bird AND the bee . . .
and (of course) with the monkey
(eating apples)
oh so high, high, HIGH up
in the old, old, OLD apple tree!

The cat (quite simply) simply
Also told me she
(quite simply) simply had to agree!
And so did HER
very, very, VERY best friend,
the oh so VERY faithful dog!

The wise old owl
with my mother (quite simply)
simply ALSO agreed!
And so did HIS very, very,
VERY best friend,
the oh so very, very, VERY
well dressed frog!

And as for me
, I thought and I thought!
And I thought, and I thought,
and I thought quite a lot. . .
ALL about what my mother had said!
And I turned her words
over and over again in my HEAD!
And THEN, I decided
that what my dear, sweet mother
had said was really, truly, absolutely,
and one hundred percent TRUE!
And then I really, truly, absolutely,
AND one hundred percent KNEW
exactly and precisely
exactly what I absolutely had to DO!

And that night as I lay in my bed,
I thought once again
about what my dear, sweet mother
(to me) had said!
And I really, truly, absolutely,
and one hundred percent KNEW,
that choosing my OWN path in my life
was exactly and precisely
what I (quite simply) simply HAD to do!
And so, I decided to choose
the path of goodness and light,
and to always do exactly and precisely
what was (quite simply) simply right!
And THEN, I slept soundly
throughout the long, long night!

"Choose your path in life wisely!"

PENELOPE DYAN

www.ingramcontent.com/pod-product-compliance
Lightning Source LLC
LaVergne TN
LVHW071652060526
838200LV00029B/437